JEWISH
SPIRITUALITY
A Brief Introduction for
CHRISTIANS

Other books by Lawrence Kushner
(all Jewish Lights)

The Book of Letters: A Mystical Hebrew Alphabet

The Book of Words: Talking Spiritual Life, Living Spiritual Talk

Eyes Remade for Wonder: A Lawrence Kushner Reader

*God Was in This Place & I, i Did Not Know:
Finding Self, Spirituality, and Ultimate Meaning*

Honey from the Rock: An Introduction to Jewish Mysticism

Invisible Lines of Connection: Sacred Stories of the Ordinary

The River of Light: Jewish Mystical Awareness

For Children

Because Nothing Looks Like God
with Karen Kushner

*The Book of Miracles: A Young Person's Guide
to Jewish Spiritual Awareness*

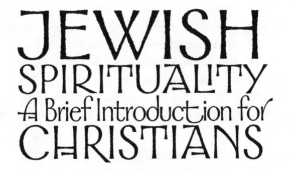

JEWISH
SPIRITUALITY
A Brief Introduction for
CHRISTIANS

Rabbi LAWRENCE KUSHNER

For People of All Faiths, All Backgrounds
JEWISH LIGHTS Publishing

Jewish Spirituality:
A Brief Introduction for Christians

© 2001 by Lawrence Kushner

Some of the material in this book is excerpted from *The Book of Miracles,* by Lawrence Kushner. Paperback Edition with illustrations by Devis Grebu, UAHC Press, New York City, New York © 1987 ISBN 0-807403-23-7. Hardcover Tenth Anniversary Edition with illustrations by Lawrence Kushner, Jewish Lights Publishing, Woodstock, Vermont © 1997 ISBN 1-879045-78-8.

For information regarding permission to reprint material from this book, please mail or fax your request in writing to Jewish Lights Publishing, Permissions Department, at the address / fax number listed below.

Library of Congress Cataloging-in-Publication Data

Kushner, Lawrence, 1943–
Jewish spirituality : a brief introduction for Christians / by Lawrence Kushner.
       p.   cm.
ISBN 1-58023-150-0 (pbk)
1. Spiritual life–Judaism. 2. Judaism–Essence, genius, nature.
I. Title.
BM723.K874 2001
296–dc21

                       2001003466

Manufactured in the United States of America

For People of All Faiths, All Backgrounds
Published by Jewish Lights Publishing
An Imprint of Turner Publishing Company
4507 Charlotte Avenue, Suite 100
Nashville, TN 37209
Tel: (615) 255-2665
www.jewishlights.com

For three men who,
by their living examples,
have taught me so much about Jesus:

Robert Trache

Basil Pennington

Jon Sweeney

CONTENTS

CONTENTS

Part Four: THE HOLY ONE

INTRODUCTION

SPIRITUALITY IS RELIGION experienced intimately. It's the core, the distilled essence of organized religion. Spirituality is where you and God meet—and what you do about it. It need not be otherworldly, pyrotechnic, angels singing Handel's "Hallelujah Chorus," spaced out, "Beam me up, Scotty," or even ethereal. Indeed, for most people, spirituality is ordinary and everyday. I suspect it may have become our word for what earlier generations called sacred or holy. The late, great mystical theologian Abraham Joshua Heschel once suggested that spirituality is life lived in the continuous presence of the divine.

Our English word *spiritual* has its roots in Greek thought and implies a split between the material world and the realm of the spirit. (The opposite of *spiritual* is *material*.) Spirituality therefore seems, almost by definition, to invite the seeker to exit this everyday, material world in order to attain some higher, spiritual or holy domain.

It is not accidental, however, that classical Hebrew lacks such a distinction. For Jewish spirituality, there is only one world that is simultaneously material *and* spiritual. To paraphrase Psalm 24:1, the whole world is full of God. Everything, from prayers to garbage, is a manifestation of God. And everything is connected and conceals the Holy One of All Being. Jewish spirituality, therefore, is an approach to life in which we strive to become aware of God's presence and purpose—even and especially in what might strike the casual observer as gross or material things.

In the words of the diesel mechanic down at Barden's Boatyard near Cape Cod, where I keep my sailboat, "Any damn fool can sail a boat in a hurricane. It takes a real sailor to make one go in no wind." We all can find the presence of God on a sunny Sunday afternoon when everything is going just right. But the evolved spiritual awareness taught by Jewish spirituality challenges us also to try to find God's presence in increasingly less obvious and unlikely places.

In the following pages I invite you to explore with me some of the rich and varied expressions of the Jewish spiritual imagination. It is a tradition that may at times, for Christians, feel strangely familiar and will, for Christians and Jews, always challenge you to see yourself and your world through a new lens.

For a Christian seeking an understanding of Jewish spirituality, the task is complicated by history. Judaism and Christianity share so much. Perhaps simply because there are so many Christians and so many varieties of Christianity, it can be easy for Christians to fall into the habit of thinking that Judaism is just another, albeit earlier, form of Christianity but without Jesus. This ultimately distorts Judaism's teaching and deprives Christians of what might be a unique and vital perspective on their own faith. In the afterword I have tried to identify some of the ways Jewish spirituality understands itself in contradistinction to Christian spirituality.

To be sure, you can only have one religion at a time. But you can, from studying another one, even from the outside, learn to see your own spiritual tradition through a new lens. The following chapters are some suggestions for how Christians might do so through the eyeglasses of the children of Israel. But first, a personal story.

My Lunch
with Jesus

What little I know about Jesus I learned from Rob. He was the one who first helped me, over a quarter century ago, understand how God might really become a person. He and I were then young clergy; he was the Episcopal priest and I was the rabbi in a small New England town. We were cautiously fascinated by each other's faith. We visited each other's place of prayer; we visited each other's home. At a Sabbath service, I even invited Rob to help me with the reading of the Torah scroll.

That Christmas Eve, as our family was about to order out for Chinese food (they were the only place open), the kitchen doorbell rang. Through the window, I could see a car with its headlights on, idling in the driveway. I opened the door; it was Robert. He was wearing his collar—a priest ready for one of Christianity's holiest of nights, a rabbi in a sweatshirt about to pick up an order of take-out food.

"Rob, what are you doing here? It's Christmas Eve. Aren't you supposed to be in church?"

"Oh, yes," he said. "We're just on our way over there now." (To me, this was like making a social call on Yom Kippur, the Jewish day of atonement!) He was holding a wrapped gift. "This was under our tree," he explained, "and it had your name on it. But

I figured, since you might not have known to look, I'd drop it off in person."

Our friendship led us to a standing monthly lunch date. We decided to write each other a one-page essay each month on the same topic. We figured it might be a personal way to learn of each other's religion in some greater depth. The topics were predictable: God, Bible, Israel, salvation. The only rule we set for ourselves was that we had to be completely candid and honest. By the sixth or seventh topic, we agreed we were ready to write about Jesus. This is what I wrote to Rob twenty-five years ago and shared with him over our lunch:

> I am wary of Jesus. Not because of anything he taught or even because of anything his disciples taught about him. (Although some of the things the author of John's gospel said about me and my people ought to be forever banned from public reading by any person who thinks loving people is important.) Whether they were mistaken or merely premature, the idea that God should at last take the form of a human being, that the yearning God and humanity share for one another should be focused in one person is a very compelling vision: Word become flesh.
>
> For millennia we Jews had tried to make it work in the other direction, from the bottom

up. Raising ourselves to the ideal of Torah's teaching. Judaism seeks to raise ordinary people to the realization of holiness, transforming flesh into word. Then came Christianity, teaching that Jesus represented an attempt to understand the yearning from the other direction. Truth be told: Neither tradition has yet succeeded.

I am wary of Jesus because of history and what so many of those who said they believed in him have done to my people. Christianity, you could say, has ruined Jesus for me. Somehow through the ages the suffering of Jesus has become confused with the suffering of the Jewish people, my people, me. That is the key to my problem with him. His death has even become causally linked with some denial on *my* part. And this in turn has been used as a justification for *my* suffering.

In this way, Jesus means for me—not the one who suffered for the world's sins, but the one *on account of whom* I must suffer. (Is there anyone who could deny the intimate relationship of Christian Europe and the Holocaust?) Most of my early learning came from Jews who were unable to conceal this hurt-become-anger and who unconsciously portrayed him as enemy.

Nevertheless, I still believe in the coming of an anointed one. A redeemer whose living example will initiate the ultimate humanism and compel even the angriest cynic into confessing that here indeed is a person in whom the eternal yearning for consciousness to behold itself has at last succeeded. The great Sinai teaching at last realized.

That's what I wrote, and that's what I handed Rob as we sat down to eat. But then something surprising and—I now understand—transforming happened. He finished the page, slowly set it down on his plate, and looked up at me. His face was ashen.

I winced, fearing that I had crossed some line, that with my smug bluntness I had injured my new friend. But to my surprise Rob only whispered, "Please forgive me, forgive us. It could not have been Jesus *those* Christians served." His eyes were moist with tears. What was more, this empathy he could not conceal seemed to grow directly from the core of his faith.

"Your religion," I said, "wants you to care about me *that* much?"

"Oh yes," he said. "Don't you see, I must continuously seek to find God in every person. Jesus is only the beginning. You, Larry, are easy. But the ultimate goal is to find my Lord within everyone—even people I like a lot less than you, even people I dislike, even ones I despise."

And then it dawned on me: So that's what it means to say that God can take the form of a human being. That event in the past, for Rob, imposed an obligation for what might happen in the future. And each human meeting is another potential opportunity toward that ultimate goal. Right here across the table from me was a truly holy man, one in whom the spirit *had* become flesh. And so together we blessed the meal we were about to share.

The following pages are my attempt to return his gift—a way to bless the nourishment we all must share together.

Lawrence Kushner

PART ONE

CREATION

THE HEAVENS REHEARSE
THE PRESENCE OF GOD...
—Psalm 19:2

Chapter 1

OPENINg YOUR EYES

WHEN THE PEOPLE OF ISRAEL crossed through the Red Sea, they witnessed what some say was the greatest miracle that ever happened. On that day they saw a sight more awesome than all the visions of the prophets combined. The sea split and the waters stood like great walls, while Israel escaped to freedom on the distant shore. Awesome. But not for everyone.

According to ancient rabbinic legend, two people, Reuven and Shimon, hurried along among the crowd crossing through the sea. But they never once looked up. They noticed only that the ground beneath their feet was still a little muddy—like a beach at low tide.

"This is terrible!" said Reuven. "There's mud all

over the place!"

"Disgusting!" said Shimon. "I'm in muck up to my ankles!"

"You know what?" replied Reuven. "When we were slaves in Egypt, we had to make our bricks out of mud, just like this!"

"Yeah," said Shimon. "There's no difference between being a slave in Egypt and being free here."

And so it went, Reuven and Shimon whining and complaining all the way across the bottom of the sea. For them there was no miracle, only mud. Their eyes were closed. Even though they walked right through it, they might as well have been asleep (*Midrash Exodus Rabba* 24.1).

People see only what they're looking for and what they understand, not necessarily what lies in front of them. For example, if you see a television set, you know what it is and how it works. But imagine someone who has never seen a television. To such a person it would only be a strange and useless box. Imagine being in a video store, filled with movies and stories and music, and not even knowing it. How sad when something is right before your eyes, but you are asleep to it. It's like that with our world, too.

Something like this once happened to Jacob. He dreamed of a ladder joining heaven and earth. Angels were climbing up and down on it, and God appeared and spoke to Jacob. When he awoke the next morning, he was shaken and said to himself, "Surely God was in this very place all along, and I didn't even know it!" (Genesis 28:16).

The medieval French commentator Rabbi Shelomo Yitzchaki, known as Rashi (after the initials of his name), explained that Jacob meant: "If I had known God would be here, then I wouldn't have gone to sleep!"

Jewish spirituality invites us to wake up and open our eyes to the myriad beautiful, mysterious, and holy things happening all around us every day. Many of them are like little miracles: when we wake up and see the morning light, when we taste food and are nourished, when we learn from others and grow wise, when we embrace people we love and receive their affection in return, when we help those around us and feel good. All these and more are there for us every day. But we must open our eyes to see them; otherwise we only wind up being like Reuven and Shimon, only able to see mud.

Suppose, right now, your eyes are closed. How do you wake up?

Chapter 2

PAYING ATTENTION

BEFORE MOSES became a leader of the Jewish people, he was a shepherd. One day, while tending his flock, he came upon a bush that was burning but was not consumed. As Moses stared at this awesome sight, God spoke to him for the first time (Exodus 3:1–6).

People usually explain that God used the burning bush to attract Moses' attention. But suppose you were God and could do anything you wanted—split the Red Sea, make the sun stand still, set up a pillar of fire. Compared with such spectacular displays, a burning bush is not very impressive. So why did God choose such a modest miracle?

Perhaps the burning bush wasn't a miracle but a test. God wanted to find out if Moses could see mystery in something as ordinary as a bush on fire. In order to see it as a miracle, Moses had to watch the flames long enough to realize that the branches were not being consumed and that something awesome was happening. Once God saw that Moses could pay attention, God spoke to him.

Much later, when God was ready to give Moses the Torah on Mount Sinai, God said, "Come up to Me on the mountain and be there" (Exodus 24:12). Rabbi Menahem Mendl Morgenstern, from the town of Kotzk in Poland (whom we call the Kotzker Rebbe), asked: "If God told Moses to come up on the mountain, then why did God also say, 'be there'? Where else would he be?" The answer, suggests the Kotzker, is that not only did God want Moses to be up on the mountain, God also wanted him to pay close attention, to be fully present. Otherwise Moses would not really be there. Often people are physically in a place, but because they are not paying attention they might as well be somewhere else.

Judaism has a unique way of remembering to pay attention. It is called a *berachah,* or a blessing. It begins, *Baruch atah Adonai,* "Holy One of blessing," *Elohenu melech ha'olam,* "Your presence fills creation." Then we add words appropriate for the occasion, like "who brings forth bread from the earth," or "who removes sleep from my eyes and slumber from my eyelids," or "who spreads the shelter of peace over us."

Each time Jews recite a blessing, they are effectively saying, "Pay attention. Something awesome is happening all around us." In this way, they realize again and again that our everyday world conceals wonders and mysteries.

Chapter 3

ONe HIDDEN EVERYWHERE

IF YOU PAY CLOSE ATTENTION, you will discover that wonders and mysteries are hidden everywhere.

The Baal Shem Tov, the founder of Hasidism (an eighteenth-century spiritual folk revival in Eastern Europe), used to tell a story about how God is concealed within the world. Once there was a king who was a master of illusion. He could make people see things that weren't really there. More than anything else, the king wanted his people to come and be close to him. But the people were always too busy. The farmers needed to milk the cows, the sailors had to scrub the decks, and the shopkeepers had to sell their wares. So the lonely king devised a plan.

He built around himself a magnificent but illusory castle. Then he sent out invitations to everyone in his kingdom: "You are personally invited to come and be close to the king. But it will not be easy; the king is hidden in a great castle."

"What a challenge," his subjects said, and they hurried to the castle. When they arrived, they found that the walls were high, the windows barred, and the gates bolted. Furthermore, in front of each entrance to the castle, the king had placed magnificent but illusory treasures. One by one, as the people arrived they settled instead for the treasures and left. "It is like that with us, too," the Baal Shem Tov would say. "We start out eagerly looking for God but get distracted easily and give up the search."

Then one day someone came along and thought, "These treasures are beautiful, but they are not why I have come. What if the walls and the gates of this castle are only an illusion?" She approached the wall, examined it closely, and saw that it was not really there! Nothing stood between herself and the king!

Like the castle, everything in the world—trees, animals, oceans, stars, even people—conceals the One who made it and reveals the One who can be found inside it. King David expressed this when he wrote in one of his psalms, "the whole world and everything in it belong to God" (Psalm 24:1).

Rabbi Menahem Nahum, from the Ukrainian town of Chernobyl, taught that we can find God's presence everywhere. "There is nothing besides the presence of God...and the presence of the Creator remains in each created thing." If you handwrite a letter for a friend, you are in the letter. If you design and build a house, your presence is in that house. If you make a gift for your lover, your presence is in that gift. We are in what we make. And, because God made the whole universe, God can be found everywhere within it.

When we say that God is everywhere, it does not mean that God is invisible. It means if we look closely, we can find God's presence hidden everywhere because God created everything. Because God is hidden in everything, all things are connected to one another.

Chapter 4

EVERYTHINg
IS CONNECTED

THE TALMUD (a twenty-volume compendium of Jewish law and lore) records the legend of a man named Honi who lived in ancient Israel. One day Honi saw an old man planting a carob tree and asked, "How long will it take for that tree to bear fruit?"

"Seventy years," replied the man.

"But you are already old; you'll never live that long!" replied Honi.

"I know," explained the man, "but my parents and grandparents planted fruit trees for me, so I am planting fruit trees for my children and my grandchildren."

Honi was very impressed by this answer. He sat down behind some nearby rocks to take a nap. When he awoke, he saw a man gathering carob fruit and asked him how it was possible for newly planted trees to yield fruit in such a short time.

"A short time?" repeated the man in disbelief. "My grandfather planted this tree!"

"Oh, my God!" thought Honi. "I have slept for seventy years!" (*Ta'anit* 22b–23a).

Each generation is linked to the next by its actions. We depend on those who came before us, just as someday our children will depend on us. For this reason, all the generations are connected to one another. In the same way generations are linked, we are also connected to all the people around us.

When the children of Israel wandered in the wilderness, they carried a portable tabernacle called the *mishkan*. Its construction required everyone's help. When the work of the *mishkan* was finally completed, the Torah says that "the tabernacle was 'one.'" (Exodus 36:13). Rabbi Mordecai Yosef Leiner of the Polish town Ishbitz was puzzled because this seems to be an odd thing to say about a building. Perhaps, he suggested, the Torah is not telling us something about the building but about its builders and how they worked.

While building the *mishkan*, all the children of Israel worked as a team. Each person, contributing only one small part, felt as important as every other person. After the *mishkan* was completed, they saw how their individual tasks fit together, as if one person had constructed the whole thing. Realizing how they had depended on one another, they understood that the tabernacle was "one." Even the person who made the Holy Ark itself (that would contain the tablets of the covenant at Sinai) realized that he was no more important than the person who only made the courtyard tent pegs.

We are joined, therefore, not only to people who have lived long before us, and who will live after we have died, but to people now living and to people we do not know. Invisible lines of depending are everywhere, as if millions of glistening threads tie us to the universe and the universe to us. Nothing is ever detached, alone. We are all parts of one great living organism.

Martin Buber, perhaps the greatest Jewish philosopher of the twentieth century, believed that nothing was more important than the relationship between two people. They can be members of the same family or sometimes even complete strangers. When two individuals realize, for even just a moment, that they depend on each other, that they are fully present for one another, that they are connected to one another, then they have come closer to God. Buber called this an I-Thou experience and imagined that the invisible lines of relation joining them to one another also join them to God.

All human beings are joined to one another, and

that "all-joined-togetherness" is an important part of God. Upon waking in the morning and upon retiring each night, Jews recite the passage from Deuteronomy 6:4 known as the *Shema*: "Hear O Israel, the Lord our God, the Lord is One." In so doing, they not only proclaim that God is One; they remind themselves that everything and everyone is connected—that it's all One. Indeed, the more we look at our world, the more we realize that it is made according to a master plan, a blueprint.

PART TWo

TORAH

SHE IS A TREE OF LIFE TO THEM
THAT HOLD FAST TO HER...
—Proverbs 3:18

Chapter 5

✝ BLUEPRINt
fo⌐ CREATION

BLUEPRINTS are written instructions for constructing a building. They show the design of the completed structure that forever remains within the building. In the same way, sheet music instructs the musician. The notes are on paper, but whenever the melody is played, they are also in the music. If you have ever tried to build a complicated model or play a song on the piano, you understand why it is necessary to have a plan before you begin.

Biologists have discovered that each person has within every cell a molecule called DNA that contains his or her genetic code. It is a personal blueprint, a plan for the body, determining the color of one's eyes, the shape of one's face, and how tall one will grow. Our universe also has such a plan.

According to a midrash in *Pirke de-Rabbi Eliezer* (one of hundreds of anthologies weaving stories and legends in and around the text of the Hebrew Bible), at the beginning of the beginning, God was unable to create the world. No matter how many times and how many different ways God tried to arrange them, the parts wouldn't fit together. The universe kept collapsing because God had no diagram, no design.

God said, "I need an overall plan for My world. I want it to be One, as I am One." For this reason, God decided to use Torah, the handwritten scroll of the Five Books of Moses, as a blueprint for creation and in that way all the parts of the world would fit together. God said, "In that way, I and My Torah will be within everything!" (*Pirke de-Rabbi Eliezer* 3).

Long ago the Rabbis of the Talmud understood this. When we read in the Book of Proverbs (8:22) that "God made me as the very first thing," the Rabbis understood *me* to mean that the Torah preceded creation. By Torah, they did not mean literally the scroll of the Torah kept in the ark in the synagogue, but an idea or a plan that God could use. They discovered this same idea when they realized that there were two ways to translate *b'ray-sheet*, the first Hebrew word in the Book of Genesis.

We usually translate *b'ray-sheet* as "In the beginning." But the Rabbis noticed that the Hebrew letter *bet* doesn't always mean "in"; it can also mean "with." If that is so, then *b'ray-sheet* (as in "In the beginning God created the heavens and the earth") also could be read as "With *ray-sheet* God created the heavens and the earth." And this would mean, suggested the Rabbis, that *ray-sheet* must be another name for Torah. In other words, God created the world with Torah. Torah is God's blueprint for the world (*Midrash Genesis Rabba* 1.1).

Another rabbinic legend says that the words of Torah are spoken continuously from Mount Sinai without interruption (*Midrash Pirke Avot* 6.2; *Midrash Exodus Rabba* 41.7). We cannot hear the voice because of the noise and distractions all around us. Even when we shut off the television and ask everyone in the room to be silent, even when we stop making sounds ourselves, the distracting "noise" of thinking still goes on inside our own heads. And that is what made Mount Sinai so special: God hushed the world to perfect silence.

When God gave the Torah, no bird chirped and no fowl flew, the wind and sea stood still, and the angels stopped singing "Holy, holy, holy." Once there was complete silence, God's voice went forth (*Midrash Exodus Rabba* 29:9). And everyone could hear the words of Torah that had been there all along.

Chapter 6

THe SILENCe of SINAI

NO ONE REALLY KNOWS for sure what happened on Mount Sinai. Some imagine that God dictated the whole Torah, word by word. Others believe that the Ten Commandments were carved in stone with the finger of God. The Torah itself actually contains conflicting accounts. Some think that in addition to the Torah, God also whispered the Talmud to Moses. Some believe that God did not speak or write; rather, God inspired Moses. And there are even those who think that Moses imagined the whole thing.

Jewish spirituality tolerates all these interpretations and more. Something as important as how God reveals God's self to people and what God says is certain to get Jews arguing. But, no matter what our interpretation, Jews all agree that what happened on Mount Sinai was a very important Jewish event.

Once several Jews were having just such an argument. The first one claimed that God gave the whole Torah, word by word. A second one said that God gave only the ten utterances, commonly called the Ten Commandments.

A third person remembered the old legend from the Talmud (*Makot* 23a–b) which tells that God didn't give ten sayings but only the first two ("I am the Lord your God..." and "You shall not have any other gods beside Me..."). "After all," that person suggested, "the first two sayings are the basis for all of Judaism. One who remembers that there is a God who frees people and that there are no other gods will probably be religious." A fourth person said that God uttered only the first utterance ("I am the Lord your God"). The four agreed that if God had given only one saying, the first would have been the most important one: that there is a God.

"No. God didn't even say that much!" insisted a fifth person. "All God said was the first word of the first saying, 'I' [in Hebrew, *anochi*]." All five then agreed that if God had said only one word, it would have been *anochi* because it affirms the importance of the self.

Then Rabbi Mendl Torum of Rymanov, who had been listening to all of this, came forward and said,

"Not even the first word. All God said was the first letter of the first word of the first utterance—which in Hebrew is also the first letter of the alphabet, *alef*."

But *alef* is not entirely silent. *Alef* is the softest yet still audible noise there can be. It is the sound the larynx makes as it clicks into gear. For this reason, *alef* is the mother of all articulate speech. Open your mouth and begin to make a sound. Stop! That is *alef*. At Sinai, all the people of Israel needed to hear was the sound of *alef*. It meant that God and the Jewish people could have a conversation.

The *Zohar*—the primary text of Kabbalah, the Jewish mystical tradition—teaches that *alef*, the almost sound of the first letter of the first word of the first saying, contains the entire Torah (*Zohar* II:85b). But not everyone hears the gentle sound of *alef*. People are able to hear only what they are ready to hear. God speaks to each of us in a personal way, taking into consideration our strength, wisdom, and preparation. In one midrash on the Book of Exodus, both Moses and his brother Aaron heard the same word from God. To Moses, it said, "Go to Egypt to free the Jews." To Aaron, who was already in Egypt, it said, "Go into the wilderness to meet your brother Moses; he needs your help."

The midrash describes God's voice as so powerful and frightening that God tempers it by creating different sounds for each person. There was even a special sounding voice just for the ears of small children (*Midrash Exodus Rabba* 5.9). The divine utterance is filled with infinite meaning. It has as many interpretations as there are people to hear it.

Chapter 7

INFINITe
UNDERSTANDING

BECAUSE WE EACH hear the words of Torah in a unique way, Jews routinely argue about their meaning. Such argument should not be misconstrued as fighting. When Jews disagree or argue about the meaning of Torah, they are actually helping one another to become better Jews.

What does it mean, for example, when the Torah says that "God created the world in six days"? Could it mean that before there was a sun or an earth, there were twenty-four-hour days just as we have now? Or does it teach that every week our world is created anew and that on Shabbat (the seventh day) we should stop creating, just as God stopped?

In Hebrew such an argument is called *l'shaym shamayim*: an argument for the sake of heaven, or an argument for God's sake (*Talmud Avot* 5.17). Trying to understand the Torah is an endless search. No matter how many times we reread it, or how many times we are sure we understand it, a new interpretation will arise to challenge our understanding.

Not even Moses himself understood everything in the Torah. According to the Talmud, when Moses went up on Mount Sinai, he found God adding some finishing touches to the Torah. God was drawing *tagin*, little decorative crowns, on some of the letters.

"What are you doing?" asked Moses. "I thought the Torah was already complete. How come you're adding those little crowns on some of the letters?"

"Centuries from now there will be students and teachers," answered God, "who will see in each little crown all kinds of wonderful laws and enchanting stories."

"May I visit those students and teachers?" asked Moses.

"Just turn around," replied God.

Moses found himself in a classroom where students were studying Torah. Invisible, Moses walked to the back row and sat down, but he was unable to understand what they were learning. After a few minutes, one of the students asked the teacher about the meaning of a certain passage. The teacher replied,

"I am not sure what these words mean, but we will study them anyway because we must try to remember everything Moses taught us."

At first Moses felt honored and proud. Then, with a troubled look on his face, he turned to God and said, "The students and teachers in this class are so wise, and yet You chose me to deliver Your Torah!"

God replied, "Not even you, Moses, can understand everything in the Torah" (*Menachot* 29b).

Every generation finds new meaning in the Torah. In trying to understand its teachings, we make ourselves better people. Jews have never found a better way of learning about God and of coming close to God. Everything we learn and everything we are as Jews comes from Torah. Nearly two thousand years ago, a teacher named Ben Bag Bag said, "Study the Torah and study it again and again, because everything you need to know is in it" (*Talmud Avot* 5.22).

Chapter 8

ORCHARD
of WORDS

HOW COULD EVERYTHING you need to know be contained in the Torah, in only five books? Long ago Jews became accustomed to understanding the Torah as if it were a beautiful orchard. From a distance you see only a field of trees. When you come closer, you see that each has leaves, blossoms, and fruit. When you come even closer, you realize that each fruit is covered by a skin. And if you are persistent and peel back the skin, your reward is a delicious treat. Now you realize that what at first seemed to be only a field of trees actually conceals layers within layers of wonderful things.

The Hebrew word for orchard is *pardes*, spelled *pey, resh, dalet, samech*. Each of these letters stands for a layer of the Torah.

The letter *pey* is the first letter of *peshat*, which refers to the simple, superficial story, the one you find if you just read the Torah quickly without much thought. When Adam disobeyed God and ate from the tree of knowledge, he was ashamed, so he hid himself (Genesis 3:8–10). That is the simple story.

The letter *resh* is the first letter of *remez*, which means "hint." If you think about a story or a word in the Torah, it usually will lead to your thinking about something else. As you wonder what the word means, you might notice that it reminds you of something you have thought about or done in the past. Perhaps, like Adam, you once did something you were ashamed of and tried to hide. Adam's story hints at something in your life.

The letter *dalet* is the first letter of *derash*, which means "interpreting." Some of the lessons in the story may remind you of other stories in the Torah that, in turn, can teach you about your life. If God knows where Adam is hiding, then why does God ask him, "Where are you?" Perhaps God wants Adam to realize that when he tries to hide from God, he is hiding only from himself.

The letter *samech* is the first letter of *sod*, which means "secret." This layer is "secret" not because it cannot be told but because, even when seen, its meaning remains mysterious. Only an advanced student of Torah can understand the "secret" meaning when God says, "Yesterday, Adam, you were so big that you extended from one end of the universe to the other, but now, after you have sinned, you can hide among the trees of the garden" (*Midrash Genesis Rabba* 19.9).

Taken all together, *pey, resh, dalet,* and *samech* (the simple, the hint, the interpreting, and the secret) spell *PaRDeS*, orchard. The Torah, the source book of Judaism, is like an orchard; it conceals many wonderful and delicious surprises. More than that, it tells us everything we need to know and do. By telling us how to live, Torah gives us life. Just as it says in the Book of Proverbs (3:18), "It is a tree of life to those who hold on to it."

PART THREE

COMMANDMENT

ALL THAT GOD HAS SPOKEN,
WE WILL DO AND WE WILL HEAR.
—EXODUS 24:7

Chapter 9

DOINg &
UNDERSTANDING

SEEING THE WONDERS of creation everywhere is one way to know about God. For Jewish spirituality, studying the words of Torah (the Five Books of Moses and, by extension, divine revelation in all its recorded forms) is another. But sometimes we are unable to see miracles, and the words of Torah appear too difficult to understand. Fortunately, there is a third way to know about God in Jewish spirituality: doing what we believe God wants us to do. But how do we know what God wants?

A curious phrase in the Book of Exodus (24:7) provides a clue. When God offers the Torah to the children of Israel, they do not say, "Let us hear what God wants, and then we'll do it." Instead, they respond in what seems to be the wrong order: "We will do and we will hear." A well-known midrash tries to explain this strange answer.

God offered the commandments, in turn, to each of the peoples of the earth.

First God went to the children of Edom and said, "Would you like My commandments?"

They said, "That depends on what they are."

"One says, 'You shall not steal,'" replied God.

"Out of the question!" the Edomites replied. "We steal all the time. It's one of the main things about being a Edomite! Give Your commandments to someone else."

When God tried the Moabites, they too insisted on first knowing what the commandments said. So God told them, "You must honor your parents."

"Impossible," said the Moabites. "Our parents are a nuisance. You can keep Your commandments."

God was crestfallen, discouraged. One by one the peoples demanded to know the commandments in advance, and one by one they refused.

Ready to give up, almost as an afterthought, God tried one last group: the children of Israel. "Would you like to have My commandments?"

"God's commandments! What an honor! That would be wonderful. We'll do whatever they say, even before we know what they are. Please, let us have them. We'll do and we'll hear" (*Midrash*

Pesikta Rabbati 21).

When Rabbi Menahem Mendl Morgenstern of Kotzk read in Exodus, "We will do and we will hear," he explained that some actions simply cannot be understood (or heard) until they are performed (or done). By doing, we understand. If the Edomites had tried not stealing or the Moabites had tried honoring their parents, they might have understood what a great treasure was being offered.

Observing the Sabbath, helping those who are less fortunate, and keeping all the other commandments (in Hebrew, *mitzvot*) in the Torah are not simply impersonal, ancient religious laws. The great German Jewish philosopher Franz Rosenzweig once explained this by making a distinction between legislation, which is simply a law written on the books, and commandment, which is something we feel is addressed to us personally. We do *mitzvot* because we believe God calls on us personally to do them.

My own teacher, Rabbi Arnold Jacob Wolf, explained this with the following metaphor: Being a Jew means you walk along a street studded with precious stones. The goal is to gather as many as you can. Each is a *mitzvah* (divine commandment, or sacred deed). Some of the jewels are easily dislodged from the pavement and put into one's knapsack. But others are more difficult to do and understand. They effectively remain stuck. It is like that with the *mitzvot.* Some, like honoring parents or helping others, are relatively easy; others, like not eating forbidden foods or not gossiping, are more difficult.

When Jews perform a *mitzvah,* we make it ours. We understand it; we "hear" it. It becomes part of us. In this way, performing a *mitzvah* changes us and brings us closer to God. These holy deeds are Judaism's way of realizing the holiness hidden everywhere and repairing creation.

Chapter 10

REP-AIRINg the WORLD

DURING THE SIXTEENTH CENTURY, in the Galilean village of Tsefat, Rabbi Isaac Luria observed that in his world, like ours, many things seemed to be wrong. People suffered from hunger, disease, hatred and war. "How could God allow such terrible things to happen?" wondered Luria. "Perhaps," he suggested, "it is because God needs our help." He explained his answer with the following mystical legend from a collection now known as Lurianic Kabbalah.

When first setting out to make the world, God planned to pour a holy light into everything to make it real. God prepared vessels to contain this light. But something went wrong. The light was so bright that the vessels burst, shattering into millions of broken pieces like dishes dropped on the floor. The Hebrew phrase that Luria used for this "breaking of the vessels" is *sh'virat ha-kaylim.*

Our world is such a mess because it is filled with broken fragments. When people fight and hurt one another, they allow the world to remain shattered. The same can also be said of people who have pantries filled with food yet allow others to starve. According to Luria, we live in a cosmic heap of broken pieces, and God cannot repair it alone.

That is why God created us and gave us freedom of choice. We are free to do whatever we please with our world. We can allow things to remain broken or, as Luria urged, we can try to repair the mess. Luria's Hebrew phrase for "repairing the world" is *tikkun olam.*

In Jewish spirituality, perhaps the most important task in life is to find what is broken in our world and repair it. The commandments in the Torah instruct us not only how to live as Jews but, in so doing, how to mend creation.

At the beginning of the Book of Genesis (2:15) we read that God put Adam and Eve in the Garden of Eden and told them not to eat from the tree of knowledge. God also told them that it was their job to take care of the garden and to protect it.

The stories in the Torah tell not only of what happened long ago but also of what happens in each generation. The stories happen over and over again in the life of each person. They are true, not because they happen*ed* but because they *happen*. The Garden of Eden is our world, and we are Adam and Eve. When God says, "Take care of the garden and protect it," God says to us, "Take care of your world and protect it."

According to one midrash, God showed Adam and Eve the Garden of Eden and said, "I have made the whole thing for you, so please take good care of it. If you wreck it, there will be no one else to repair it other than you" (*Midrash Ecclesiastes Rabba* 7.13).

Jewish spirituality is eminently practical, even behaviorist: When you see something that is broken, fix it. When you find something that is lost, return it. When you see something that needs to be done, do it. In that way, you will take care of your world and repair creation. If all the people in the world were to do so, our world would truly be a Garden of Eden, the way God meant it to be. If everything broken could be repaired, then everyone and everything would fit together like the pieces of one gigantic jigsaw puzzle. But for people to begin the great task of repairing creation, they must realize the awesome power God has put into their hands.

Chapter 11

THe HANDS of GOD

THERE IS AN ANCIENT STORY from the land of Israel about the richest man in town. He was sleeping (as usual) through Sabbath morning worship. Every now and then, the rich man would almost wake up, trying to get comfortable on the hard wooden bench, and then sink back into a deep sleep. One morning he awoke just long enough to hear the chanting of the Torah verses from Leviticus 24:5-6, in which God instructs the children of Israel to place twelve loaves of *challah* (twisted egg bread) on a table in the ancient wilderness tabernacle.

When services ended, the wealthy man woke up, not realizing that he had only heard a few verses from the Torah being chanted about how God wanted twelve loaves of *challah*. Convinced instead that God had come to him in his sleep and personally asked him to bring twelve loaves of *challah* as an offering to God, he felt honored that God should single him out. But he also felt a little foolish. Of all the things God could want from such an important person, twelve loaves of *challah* didn't seem very important. But who was he to argue with God? So, he went home and baked the bread.

Upon returning to the synagogue, he had a new problem: how to get the bread to God? He decided the only proper place for such a holy gift was with the Torah scrolls in the ark. He carefully arranged the loaves and said to God, "Thank You for telling me what You want." (To tell someone you love what you want is itself a gift.) "Pleasing You fills me with delight." Then he left.

No sooner had he gone than the poorest Jew in the town, the synagogue caretaker, entered the sanctuary. All alone, he poured out his heart before God. "O Lord, I am so poor. My family is starving; we have nothing to eat. Unless You perform a miracle for us, we will surely perish." Then, as was his custom, he walked around the room to tidy it up. When he ascended the *bimah* (raised platform at the front of the room) and opened the ark, there before him were twelve loaves of *challah*! "A miracle!" exclaimed the poor man. "I had no idea You worked like that! Blessed are You, O God, who answers our prayers." Then he ran home to share the good news and the bread with his family.

Minutes later, the rich man returned to the sanctuary, curious to know whether or not God really ate *challah*. Slowly he ascended the *bimah*, and opened the ark. The loaves were gone. "Oh, my God!" he whispered, "You really ate the loaves! I thought You were just kidding. This is wonderful. You can bet that next week I'll bring another twelve loaves—and with raisins in them, too!"

The following week, the rich man brought a dozen loaves to the synagogue and reverently placed them in the ark. Only minutes later, the poor man entered the sanctuary. "God, I don't know how to say this, but I'm out of food again. We ate some, we sold some, and we managed to give some to charity. But now, nothing is left—and unless, in Your infinite mercy, You do another miracle, we will starve." He approached the ark and slowly opened its doors. "Another miracle!" he cried. "Twelve more loaves— and with raisins, too! Thank You, God; this is wonderful!"

The *challah* exchange became a weekly ritual. It went on for twenty years. And, as with many rituals that become routine, after a time neither man gave it much thought. Then, one day, the rabbi, detained in the sanctuary longer than usual, saw this amazing sight: the richest man in town ran in and put a dozen loaves of *challah* in the ark. As soon as he left, the poorest man in town ran in and took them away.

Whereupon the rabbi summoned the two men together and scolded them for what they had been doing.

"Shame on you both," he said. "Don't you know that to ascribe corporeality to God violates a fundamental tenet of Judaism. God doesn't eat *challah*. And God doesn't bake *challah*."

"Oh, I see," said the rich man sadly.

"Now I understand," said the poor man.

"Maybe we shouldn't do it any more," they both said.

"No," counseled the rabbi. "Each of you, look at your hands. Yours," he said turning to the rich man, "are the hands of God giving food to the poor. And yours," said the rabbi to the poor man, "also are the hands of God, receiving gifts from the rich. God can still be present in your lives. Continue baking and continue taking. Your hands are the hands of God."

Indeed, not only are we all agents of God, we are, each one of us, present within the divine.

Chapter 12

DRAWING CLOSE

THE COLLECTED LIFE TEACHINGS of Rabbi Yehuda Aryeh Lieb of the Polish town of Ger are named the *Sefas Emes* ("Straight Talk"). They are considered the crowning achievement of Polish Hasidism. The *Sefas Emes* teaches that not only is God hidden everywhere throughout all creation, but we can also bring this concealed holiness out into the open through our performance of sacred deeds (*Shelah Lekah* 5632).

Indeed, doing so is the reason we were created — to be agents fulfilling the will of our Creator. The same Rabbi cites a midrash (*Numbers Rabba* 16:1) teaching that nothing is more beloved before God than someone sent to do a holy deed who gives his or her heart and soul over to the task. But in order to give yourself over completely to the sacred deed, you must be willing to lose—not your life, hopefully, but your self. You must be willing to allow it to dissolve like a drop of water fallen into the ocean, so that it is no longer recognizable as a separate or discrete thing. Such a spiritual loss of self and fusion with the divine is called *devekut*. It is a "momentary nothing-ness" in which it is no longer possible to know where you (or, for that matter, anything) ends or begins. It is not glazed over, empty-headed, or zoned out. The borders of your self are erased. All that remains now instead is the unity of all being. You realize that you are (and indeed have always been) present *within* the divine! It's all God!

Obviously, you cannot set *devekut* as your goal. No matter how hard you try, *devekut* always comes as an undeserved gift from on High. The idea is simply to serve God with all your heart, and some-times, in devoting yourself to that holy service, you are rewarded with losing your self. You are so fully absorbed and present in what you are doing that you don't even have time to realize that it's you who's doing it. In this way, through everything you do—even ordinary, everyday actions—you can bring holiness into the world. Everything you do is *l'shaym shamayim*, for the sake of heaven.

When Moses is on Mount Sinai he begs to be

able to see God, but God only replies that a person cannot see God and live. "Instead," God says, "I will set you in a cleft of the rock, and after I have passed by you will be able to see My back." The Hebrew for "My back" is *achorai*. We miss the whole point, however, if we read it literally and imagine that God has a back. The word *achor* also has a temporal sense. What God seems to be saying to Moses is that you can see "My afterward" (Exodus 33:23). You can see what it's like just after I've been there. But if you knew what it was like while I was there, that would mean you were still hanging on to a little piece of your self-awareness that was telling you it was you who was there. And that would also mean there was a part of your consciousness detached and watching the whole thing, and therefore not *all of you* was there. There are, in other words, simply some things in life that demand such total self-absorption that you cannot even know it's you who is there until it's over. Being in the presence of God is such an experience.

Rabbi Levi Yitzhak of Berditchev offers another comment on this same scene. He notices an apparent redundancy in Exodus 34:6. The text reads: "And the Lord passed before him and proclaimed, 'The Lord, the Lord, compassionate and gracious, slow to anger, abounding in kindness and faithfulness...'" The reason the words "the Lord" are repeated, explains Levi

Yitzhak, is that the human soul is a part of God, and when the soul calls out to God, one dimension of God is, as it were, calling out to another. In this way, when you experience the presence of God, you are overwhelmed with reverence and love. And at that moment, God is calling to God! We realize that we are part of what we seek to observe.

PART FOUR
THe HOLY ONE

HEAR O ISRAEL, THE LORD IS
OUR GOD, THE LORD IS ONE.
−Deuteronomy 6:4

Chapter 13

THe SELF
of the UNIVERSe

TALKING ABOUT GOD can lead to confusion and contradiction: God is like a person but has no body. God is everywhere but dwells in heaven.

One insight of Jewish spirituality is this: The reason we find talking about God so difficult is that we are part of what we are trying to understand. We cannot separate ourselves completely from God, and therefore we can never comprehend the totality. It would be like trying to look at our own eyes without a mirror.

The first tractate of the Talmud considers what King David meant in the Book of Psalms (103:1) when he said, "Bless the Lord, O my soul."

King David must have been referring to his innermost self. Just as God fills the whole world, so the self fills the body. Just as God sees but is not seen, so the self sees but is not seen. Just as God nourishes the whole world, so the self nourishes the whole body. Just as God dwells in the innermost part of everything, so the self dwells in the innermost part of each person (*Berachot* 10a). This does not mean that God is the universe or that we are God. Rather, God is the Self of the universe.

Professor Richard Rubenstein once explained that God is like the ocean and we are like the waves. The waves seem to be separate from the ocean, rising and falling on their own. But even though they seem to be separate, the waves are always *made* of the ocean; they never exist apart from it. Of course, the ocean is more than the total of all the waves, but we can nevertheless learn a lot about it from watching the waves. In the same way, we learn most of what we know about God from people.

Another way of thinking about God is to imagine that God is like a river made of light, flowing softly within all creation. In the Book of Psalms (36:10), King David says, "God, You are the fountain of life; by Your light do we see light." Since we are made of this light, we cannot see it. But it flows within us, joining us with everything in the universe.

The most important thing we can say about God is that "God is One." As it says in Deuteronomy 6:4, "Hear, O Israel: the Lord is our God, the Lord is One!"

This is much more than the rejection of polytheism. When we say the *Shema*, we remind ourselves that all of creation, in all its myriad forms—mountains and dirt, songs and silence, human beings and microscopic organisms, everything—all are manifestations of one great underlying unity. The Holy One of Being. The Only One of Being. It's all God—even the parts we do not like or understand.

Chapter 14

THe WHIRLWIND

IF GOD DWELLS within all creation, then God is what life is made of. For this reason, when we are keenly aware of being alive, we also feel God's presence. We sense a special closeness to God when someone is born, just as we do when someone dies. This does not necessarily mean that God causes people to be born or to die.

The ways of God are beyond human understanding. Only the experience of living can begin to give some insight. Simple formulas, such as the thought that good people will be rewarded and bad people will be punished, often do not hold true in real life. Likewise, childhood metaphors like the notion of a God "up in heaven" running things seem inadequate.

The Book of Job teaches us about suffering and the mystery of knowing God. Job is the story of a righteous man whose happy life suddenly turns miserable. His business fails, his children die, and he is afflicted with terrible diseases.

Despite his ordeal, Job never curses God. His friends believe that bad things happen only as God's punishment for sin, that Job suffers because he must have done something wrong. They try to convince him to apologize to God, but Job refuses, knowing he has acted justly. Heartbroken and angry, he sits alone on a pile of ashes, wishing he had never been born.

Finally, at the very end of the book, from out of a whirlwind, God asks Job one question after another: "Where were you when I laid the foundations of the universe? Have you commanded the morning to begin? Have you entered the bottom of the ocean? Do you know the way to the home of light? If you know, tell Me" (Job 38:4,12,16,17,18). Job realizes that he knows very little about the mysteries of creation and that it is awesome simply to be alive. Now he understands that God is present in everything—even things he does not understand or like. Suddenly he feels grateful just to be able to love, to learn, and to live. Once that happens, the blessings and the fullness of his life are restored.

Becoming an ethically mature adult includes

understanding that bad people often go unpunished and good people are often not rewarded. Instead, the way we feel when we do bad things is its own punishment and the way we feel when we do good is its own reward. To be sure, we stand guilty or innocent before our Creator. But God is not in the reward-and-punishment business. It is the same way with a spiritual approach to life. God seems to say, "Try to make your world the way I have taught you, and that will bring you more happiness than the greatest reward." We emerge from an awareness of the presence of God with a heightened yearning to be better people.

Chapter 15

PRAYING
GOD'S PRAYERS

RABBI DOV BAER, the great storyteller *(Magid)* of the Polish town Mezritch, used to say that a person is like a *shofar* (ram's horn, sounded on the Jewish New Year as a ritual of awakening). A *shofar* sounds only when breath is blown through it; we can say prayers only because God moves through us.

Like God, the prayers are everywhere, but they need mouths and hands to give them melody and movement. Without us they would flow unnoticed through the universe. People are the instruments that transform prayers into music and words.

The Book of Psalms is one of our biggest and oldest collections of prayer-poems. Its words, like the words of other prayers in the traditional Jewish prayer book, are a script or a musical score for words and songs that already exist within each of us and within all creation. One Psalm verse (104:24), for example, reads, "How awesome is what You do, God; You have made everything with wisdom; the earth is full of Your creations." These words, recited for generations, are already in the universe, whether or not we say them. If we say them, however, we understand a little more about the mystery of being alive.

Sometimes the prayers seem to come from our own heart; at other times we find them written in the prayer book; at still other times they seem to be whispered by the wind. But, no matter where we find them, the words of prayers are already present. They need someone to speak them. By giving them a voice, we come closer to God.

Rabbi Kalonymos Kalmish Shapiro of Piesetzna, who died in the Holocaust, taught that "not only does God hear our prayers, but God also says our prayers through us as well." God's words become ours.

Praying connects us to God, and since God is the One through whom every one and every thing is connected to all the others, prayer joins us to all creation. Abraham Joshua Heschel, one of the great spiritual teachers of the twentieth century, explained that in prayer, we realize that our "self is not the hub, but the spoke of the revolving wheel." Such a feeling is so important that Jews devote an entire day of every week to it.

Chapter 16

BEING HERe

A SCROLL OF THE TORAH is written in Hebrew and without vowels. We have to fill in the vowels mentally as we read. Someone who understands Hebrew and has a rough idea of the story can usually easily figure out the vowels, but occasionally a word appears that can be read in different ways, depending on the vowels we add.

Such a word occurs in Genesis 2:1. The letters *vav, yod, chaf, lamed, vav* are usually given vowels so that they are pronounced *vaye'chu-lu*, which means "were finished." Taken in this manner, the verse reads: "The heavens and the earth *were finished...*"

In the Talmud, however, Rabbi Hamnuna notices that by the addition of different vowels, the letters *vav, yod, chaf, lamed, vav* could also be pronounced *vaye'cha-lu*, which means "and they finished." Taken in this manner, the verse reads: "*And they finished* the heavens and the earth" (*Shabbat* 119b).

But this raises another question: Who were the "they" who finished the heavens and the earth? Rabbi Hamnuna says that the "they" refers to God and people. Not only do we help God by caring for and repairing creation, we also join God on every Friday evening, the eve of Sabbath, by finishing our work. We say as we commence the Sabbath eve table liturgy, "God, just as you finished your work of creation, so do we stop doing our own weekday tasks."

Why is it so important to be finished? Perhaps because every unfinished task—from household chores to building a house, from someone we need to forgive to someone we need to remind we love—demands a piece of our attention. Such a task coaxes us to be back in yesterday, worrying about what we didn't finish, or it wants us to be already in tomorrow, worrying about what we still need to do. And whenever we are back in yesterday or already in tomorrow, we are not fully here. Our bodies are obviously present, but our attention is somewhere else.

To properly observe the Sabbath, therefore, we must either finish our work, as God did, or say to ourselves, "Even though it's not done, I'm going to pretend it's done anyway." On the Sabbath, I refuse to worry about what I didn't finish yesterday or what I'll need to do tomorrow; instead, I'm just going to be right here. Each week, on the Sabbath I will remind myself to savor how sweet it is to simply be where I am, remaining in the present, opening my eyes to the wonder and miracle of creation.

The story is told of a man named Isaac who lived in Cracow. He was very poor, so when he dreamed three times in a row about a great treasure buried under a bridge in the distant city of Prague, he set out on a journey to find it. But when he arrived in Prague, he discovered that the place he had seen in his dream was patrolled day and night by the king's guards. He circled the spot, watching it from a distance, until finally the guards noticed him. When the captain called to Isaac and demanded to know what he was doing there, Isaac told him about the dream.

"You mean to tell me that you believe in such dreams!" laughed the captain. "If I believed in them, I would have to go all the way to Cracow and find some man named Isaac, because I have dreamed that a great treasure lies buried beneath his bed!" Isaac thanked the captain, returned home, pushed aside his bed, and dug up the treasure that had been there all along.

What we are seeking is not in the past or in the future. It is not far away or in the possession of someone else. It is exactly where we are—and every seventh day, on the Sabbath, the miracles of creation can be ours.

Chapter 17

RETURNING HOME

OVER TWENTY YEARS AGO, Rev. Robert Trache invited me to co-teach a three-day seminar for Jews and Christians at an Episcopal retreat center in North Carolina. For a format, we selected a half dozen classic religious ideas that we would then each present to the interfaith group from Jewish and Episcopal perspectives. Most of our subjects were predictable and simple. But when Rob wanted to include Jesus, I initially found myself at a loss—until I remembered *teshuva*.

Teshuva is usually translated as "repentance," but it also can mean "answer," "apology," and above all "return"—as in going back to who you meant to be, returning home, returning to your Source. *Teshuva* is the dominant theme during the ten days between Rosh Hashanah (the Jewish New Year, a day of awakening) and Yom Kippur (the day of atonement and asking forgiveness) in the early fall. But *teshuva* is also possible and commanded throughout the entire year. And that is where Jesus comes in. If I am not mistaken, you can read any of the following statements about *teshuva* and substitute "(believing in) Jesus Christ" without making any but grammatical errors.

- *Teshuva* is the gesture of returning to God, of going home, or going back to your ultimate source.

- *Teshuva* is the letting go of your arrogance, waywardness, and sinfulness and once again placing your trust in God.

- *Teshuva* is filled with joy. It is the soul's fulfillment and even perhaps its apotheosis.

- *Teshuva* is a prerequisite for the creation of the world. God could not make the world stand until God added to it the possibility of *teshuva*.

- Without *teshuva*, the world could not endure.

- *Teshuva* is the easiest thing in the world: all that is necessary for the process of *teshuva* to begin is for the thought to occur to you.

- *Teshuva* is also the means of the world's salvation: to fully return to God would repair all creation and bring the Messiah.

- *Teshuva* is the possibility that even the most degenerate sinner can be reunited with God. Indeed, according to tradition, someone who has strayed and made *teshuva* is more beloved by God than someone who has *never* sinned.

- Finally, in the words of Rabbi Abraham Isaac Kook, "The perception of truth is the basis of *teshuva*."

Jewish spirituality teaches that the world endures because of this ever-present yearning and gesture of returning. In the words of the Talmud, "Returning home is the hardest thing in the world, for to truly return home would mean to bring the Messiah (*Yoma* 86a–b). Returning home is also the easiest thing, for all it has to do is occur to you to return home and you have already begun."

As Rabbi Abraham Isaac Kook, one of the great mystics of the twentieth century, taught, "through returning home all things are reunited with God.... Returning home is, in essence, an effort to return to one's original status, to the source of life and higher being in their fullness; without limitation and diminution, in their highest spiritual character, as illumined by the simple, radiant divine light (*Orot HaTeshuva* 4:2; 12:9).

You might say, in the language of computers, that making *teshuva* is the equivalent of clicking the reset button on your computer, the one that promises "Restore Default Configuration." This going back to our Source is a great longing that flows through and animates all creation. Through apology, repair, and attempting to heal damage done, we effectively rewrite the past. What was once a thoughtless or even wicked act, when set within the present constellation of meaning, becomes the commencement of an even greater healing.

Perhaps this is why Jews are bidden to make *teshuva*, not just on Yom Kippur but on every Sabbath, because through it, we are able to heal and perfect the past week and join God in saying of all creation, "Behold, it is good."

Obviously, accepting Jesus is more than doing *teshuva*, and doing *teshuva* is more than accepting Jesus. But the parallels go on and on. To be sure, in Judaism, the rich, corporeal, and personal christological legend is absent. Here, as in so many other instances, Judaism teaches Jews to go it without any imagery, form, or mythology. But the urge, the gesture, and the goal for Christians and Jews are surprisingly similar.

In the family album, or in one of those little frames that stands upright on an end table in your mother's apartment, is a photograph of you when you were a child. You have come a long way since those days, in many beautiful ways and in a few disappointing and perhaps even shameful ones. If you were given a time machine, is there anything you would like to tell the child in the photo who once was you? Just looking at who you were seems to awaken the possibility that you could go back to that time and, if not relive your life, at least begin again. Just this is the beginning of the return: *teshuva*. And Jewish spirituality is a way to do that with every breath.

-AFTERWORD

THERE ARE MANY FINE TEXTS on Judaism and Christianity that detail the similarities and differences between the two spiritual traditions. What follows, therefore, is only a very short list of some of Judaism's unique ways of understanding our spiritual condition, which many Christians might not realize and might confound their attempts to understand Jewish spirituality.

———•———

The primary spiritual symbol in Judaism is what Jews call *Torah*: Hebrew for the handwritten parchment scroll of the Five Books of Moses. It represents the awesome possibility that God can (and does) communicate with people. Its very existence means that the Infinite and Eternal can touch the finite and temporal without either destroying the other. Indeed, you might say that the Jewish people are brought into being with the giving of the Torah at Mount Sinai and that they renew themselves again and again through studying, interpreting, and even arguing over what it means.

This reverence for sacred text(s) should not be confused with a literalist understanding of the biblical text. The Torah is much more than the first five books of the Hebrew Bible. Most Jews have an open and even playful approach to interpreting and understanding the Bible, and this can be surprising or confusing to some Christians. For this reason, most Jewish teaching—even to the present day—begins with the texts of divine revelation. Gershom Scholem, the master historian of Jewish mysticism, once observed that in a revealed tradition like Judaism (since everything worth knowing has already been revealed by God at Mount Sinai), all creativity must therefore masquerade as commentary. No one, in other words, can have anything genuinely new worth saying; we can only have increasingly clever and subtle ways of reviewing the sacred text(s).

The very existence
of Torah is a tangible symbol of the love and intimacy between God and the Jewish people.

Christianity, for its own purposes, often mistakenly understands Torah as *nomos,* or law. But a more accurate translation would be "teaching" or simply "way." Torah is the sacred story and way of God and the Jewish people. Like any long-term, loving relationship, it has its ups and downs, romance and disappointments. When Jews see the scroll of the Torah in the ark at the front of every Jewish house of prayer, they see a memento of the time when they stood before God at Sinai, a tangible reminder of God's love for Israel. In the words of Proverbs 3:18, "She is a tree of life to them that hold fast to her." It is hardly surprising, then, that when the scroll is paraded through the congregation before its public reading, Jews customarily will reach out to touch and kiss it.

God, of course, in Judaism has neither mythology nor family. God is not born, nor does God die. God has *no* personal history. And God has no form whatsoever. I was reminded of this not long ago by a nine-year-old. I was reading the mail in my office at the synagogue when the fourth-grade teacher came running in. "Rabbi, we need you right away," she said. "They're talking about God!" I went down to the classroom and began my emergency lesson. "Tell me what you know about God for sure," I asked them. A few hands slowly went up.

"God made the world," said one.

I wrote, "Made the world" on the board.

"God's one," said another. I put that on the board, too.

"God's good," ventured a third. There were a few dissenting votes, but the majority was still for divine beneficence.

Then another child said, "God's invisible." I started to write it on the board, but another objected.

"You're wrong. God's visible. He's [sic] right here, right now."

"Oh yeah, I don't see Him," replied the first child. "What's He look like?"

To which the other said, "That's just it...there's nothing to see!"

Judaism is so intent on the imagelessness of God that we even shy away from legitimate and reasonable human heroes. In the traditional *Haggadah*, the story-liturgy for the Passover *seder* (a festive meal rehearsing and celebrating Israel's going free from Egyptian slavery), the name of Moses is not even once mentioned!

———•———

Judaism also has no dogma, no catalogue of beliefs. One's Judaism is not a matter of what you believe. Instead, it is organized around sacred deeds *(mitzvot)*. Indeed, Jews find Christianity's preoccupation with belief strange. Jews think that you can't help what you believe. To make matters even more confusing, one's Jewish identity (whether or not you are a Jew) has virtually nothing to do with what you believe. (Unless you believe that Jesus is your personal savior, in which case you have taken a giant step toward becoming a Christian.) Being a Jew is entirely a matter of being born a Jew or choosing to become one of the Jewish people through a ceremony of conversion.

In modern America, this can lead to some mind-bending identity questions. There's an old joke about a transatlantic flight of El Al (the national airline of Israel). Midway over the Atlantic, a terrorist jumps up with a machine gun, points it at the cabin full of terrified passengers, and shouts, "Who is a Jew?" Whereupon one little old man in seat 34-C says, "That's a very interesting question..."

Judaism is not a world-conquering spiritual tradition. To be sure, we welcome converts and (most of us, anyway) think we have a pretty good thing. But our success as Jews is not indexed to the number of non-Jews we persuade to join us. Whether or not there are a lot of Jews or just a few is God's business; ours is trying to live according to God's way. For this reason, most Jews find the frequent missionary attempts to convert Jews unintelligible and insulting.

A Christian colleague of mine once supplied me

with a mischievous question he advised me to put to any Christian before entering into a religious conversation. "Just ask him or her if there is anything you now lack as a Jew that you'd get if you accepted Jesus. And if he or she says anything other than 'Absolutely nothing at all,' don't waste your time. They secretly think they have a religion but that your Judaism is somehow deficient, unfinished, incomplete."

Judaism is, in other words, a complete, self-contained religion; it needs nothing—not the New Testament, Jesus, fewer laws, or anything else to complete it. (For classical Judaism, the coming of the Messiah would not "complete" Judaism; it would bring an end to history and resolve every problem for every religion and every person.)

Even though Judaism and Christianity share much, each tradition has obviously grown off in its own direction. The mere fact that we began in the same neighborhood does not mean that we therefore know all about each other. What we originally shared, when viewed now through the lens of centuries, has come to mean often radically different things. Jews find the usually well-intentioned Christian borrowing of Jewish religious practices such as a *seder* meal or lighting a Hanukkah menorah (a nine-branch candelabrum) as unintelligible and even offensive. It would be equivalent for Jews to say, "Oh yes, we love Christianity—we do our own little Eucharist, too!" Religions, my teacher Rabbi Arnold Jacob Wolf used to teach, are like spouses: they want all of you and don't coun-tenance sharing you with anyone else.

Finally, Judaism, in contradistinction to Christianity, tends to be much more oriented to this world. To be sure, there have always been many Jews who believed in one form of afterlife or another. But even for them, the importance of life after death is relatively minor in their overall Jewish outlook. Jews are primarily concerned about whether or not they are living in accordance with the teachings and the way of Torah. To do so is not only supremely fulfilling and what God wants of us; it is therefore its own reward. All this leads to a heightened reverence for life in *this* world. One of my colleagues, Rabbi Daniel Polish, explains it this way: When you die, they set you up in a big easy chair in front of a four-foot screen with quadraphonic sound. Then they begin to slowly play—over and over again—a video, depicting in minute detail *everything* you ever did in your life. Heaven or hell? You pick. Our eternal reward or our eternal punishment, in other words, is nothing more or less than this life forever and ever. So, decide now what you want for eternity!

Our focus on this world leads us to look for holiness in the here and now, and even in what less discerning observers might call ordinary or grossly material things. This world and everything in it is a manifestation of God's presence. Our challenge and goal is to find it and then act in such a way as to help others find it too.

SUGGESTIONS for FURTHER READING

1. Buber, Martin. HASIDISM AND MODERN MAN, ed. and trans. Maurice Friedman. Atlantic Highlands, N.J.: Humanities Press International, 1988, [1958].

   Six short essay-meditations on the spiritual life; a masterpiece describing virtually all the elements of a life lived in the continuous presence of God.

2. ———. TALES OF THE HASIDIM: THE EARLY MASTERS (1947); THE LATER MASTERS (1948), translated by Olga Marx. New York: Schocken, 1991.

   A collection of stories about Hasidic rebbes (spiritual masters) elucidating the primary ideas of Hasidic (and contemporary Jewish) spirituality.

3. Green, Arthur and Barry W. Holtz, eds. YOUR WORD IS FIRE: THE HASIDIC MASTERS ON CONTEMPLATIVE PRAYER. Woodstock, Vt.: Jewish Lights Publishing, 1993.

   An anthology of poetic translations of meditations on the experience of being present for (and within) the divine.

4. Scholem, Gershom G. ON THE KABBALAH AND ITS SYMBOLISM, trans. Ralph Manheim. New York: Schocken, 1965.

   A work of serious scholarship by the master historian of Jewish mysticism replete with dazzling insights into the nature of the Jewish spiritual imagination.

5. Heschel, Abraham Joshua. THE SABBATH: ITS MEANING FOR MODERN MAN. New York: Farrar, Straus & Giroux, 1995.

   An extended essay on the spiritual dimension of what is perhaps the central religious observance of contemporary Jews.

6. Matlins, Stuart M., ed. THE JEWISH LIGHTS
   SPIRITUALITY HANDBOOK: A GUIDE TO
   UNDERSTANDING, EXPLORING & LIVING A
   SPIRITUAL LIFE. Woodstock, Vt.: Jewish Lights
   Publishing, 2001.
   *Rich, creative material from over 50 spiritual
   leaders on every aspect of Jewish spirituality today:
   prayer, meditation, mysticism, study, rituals, spe-
   cial days, the everyday, and more.*

7. Steinsaltz, Adin. THE THIRTEEN PETALLED
   ROSE. New York: Basic Books, 1980.
   *An easy introduction to Jewish mystical thinking
   by the great contemporary Israeli Talmudist and
   mystic.*

8. Spiegel, Sholom. THE LAST TRIAL: ON THE
   LEGENDS AND LORE OF THE COMMAND TO
   ABRAHAM TO OFFER ISAAC AS A SACRIFICE.
   Woodstock, Vt.: Jewish Lights Publishing, 1993.
   *An elegant and literary example of the way Jews
   read and interpret one pivotal chapter of Genesis.*

CPSIA information can be obtained
at www.ICGtesting.com
Printed in the USA
JSHW022050150323
38990JS00004B/530

9 781580 231503